Sharing

M000019394

WITH BEAUTY
BEFORE ME

An Inspirational Guide for Nature Walks

By Joseph Cornell

Dawn Publications

To my dear friend, J. Donald Walters,
whose life and teaching have transformed my own.

Photographs by Robert Frutos except as indicated on page 68

Library of Congress Cataloging-in-Publication Data
Cornell, Joseph Bharat.
  With beauty before me : an inspirational guide for nature walks / by
Joseph Cornell.-- 1st ed.
    p. cm. -- (Sharing nature pocket guide ; 1)
  Includes bibliographical references.
  ISBN 1-58469-012-7
  1. Nature--Psychological aspects. I. Title.
BF353.5.N37 C67 2000
155.9'1--dc21
00-009589

Dawn Publications
12402 Bitney Springs Rd.
Nevada City, California 95959
(800) 545-7475
email: nature@dawnpub.com
website: www.dawnpub.com

Printed in United States of America
9 8 7 6 5 4 3 2
First edition

Design and computer production by Andrea Miles

In every walk with Nature one receives far more than he seeks.

—*John Muir*

CONTENTS

A Note from the Author

*T*he idea for this book came from one of my most popular nature-awareness activities, The Trail of Beauty. In this activity, people walk along a beautiful path while looking at inspiring quotations and feeling a sense of communion with the world around them. All the quotations encourage a sense of serenity and loving interaction with nature.

After every Trail of Beauty experience, people eagerly ask for copies of the quotations to use on their own walks. I wrote this book to make these wonderful and inspiring quotations available to a wider audience.

As I have arranged them, the first quotations help create a receptive mood. Many of the ones that follow include a simple, meditation-like activity; the activity will help you dive deeper into the truth of the quotation, and give you your own uplifting experiences of nature.

The title, With Beauty Before Me, comes from a Navajo poem. To the Navajo people, beauty also means the harmony that runs through life. On your walks in nature, may you always feel the unity and joy that all life shares.

Joseph Cornell
Nevada City, California
April, 2000

How to Use This Book

*A*s you walk, read and reflect on the quotations and activities, feeling also the inspiration from the natural beauty around you. Remain with each thought for a while, and reflect on its inner meaning for as long as you wish.

I encourage you to spend extra time with the activities in the Special Nature Experiences section. These experiences will help you go even more deeply into your awareness of nature. I also encourage first-time readers to start at the beginning.

The Notes pages at the end of the book are provided for you to write down your thoughts and inspirations.

One:
THE TRAIL OF BEAUTY

The real voyage of discovery
consists not in seeking new lands,
but in seeing with new eyes.

—*Marcel Proust*

Wisdom begins with wonder.

—*Socrates*

And wonder begins with humility. Only in humility can we truly see Nature's beauty and discover its secrets.

Wisdom does not inspect,
but behold.

—Henry David Thoreau

Science and the intellect describe what Nature is. Intuition, or calm feeling, enables us to perceive it fully.

The hours when the mind
is absorbed by beauty
are the only hours
when we really live . . .

—*Robert Jefferies*

16

There are two ways to live,
one is as though nothing
is a miracle. The other is
as if everything is.

—*Albert Einstein*

Pretend that you are seeing everything around you for the first time. See in each thing, life's incredible mystery and unique purpose.

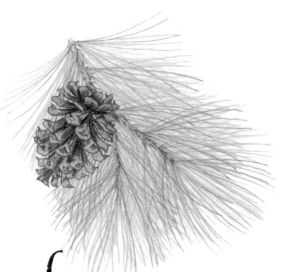

Contemplate beauty in the world
around you, and you yourself will
become beautiful.

— J. Donald Walters

With beauty before me, May I walk
With beauty behind me, May I walk
With beauty above me, May I walk
With beauty below me, May I walk
With beauty all around me,
May I walk
Wandering on a trail of beauty,
Lively I walk.

—Navajo Indians

Walk and silently repeat this Navajo chant.
Feel the beauty you see all around you. To the
Navajo, "beauty" also means harmony.

The best and most beautiful things in the world cannot be seen or even touched. They must be felt with the heart.

—*Helen Keller*

If you love it enough,
anything will talk with you.

—*George Washington Carver*

Closely look at a plant or animal. Discover its special qualities, then offer your love and appreciative thoughts to it.

24

One fancies a heart like our own must be beating in every crystal and cell. No wonder when we consider that we all have the same Father and Mother.

—*John Muir*

Muir said that at times, every cell and atom seemed to be vibrating with music and life.

O these vast, calm, measureless
mountain days . . .
Days in whose light everything
seems equally divine,
opening a thousand windows to
show us God.

—*John Muir*

Holy Earth Mother,
the trees and all nature are witnesses
of your thoughts and deeds.

—*Winnebago Indian prayer*

Silently repeat this Winnebago prayer of reverence for the earth and its Creator. Whenever an animal, plant, rock, or beautiful scene draws your attention, stop and offer silent thanks for the joy and beauty you feel.

Man is not himself only . . .
He is all that he sees;
all that flows to him
from a thousand sources . . .
He is the land,
the lift of its mountain lines,
the reach of its valleys.

—Mary Austin

To expand your consciousness,
concentrate on the distances of your
environment.

—*J. Donald Walters*

We are in the mountains,
and the mountains are in us ...
Wonderful how completely
everything in wild nature fits into us ...
The Sun shines not on us, but in us.
The rivers flow not past,
but through us...

—John Muir

*B*reathe in the fresh air surrounding you. Exhale and observe the flow of air around you. Follow it as it passes through nearby trees and over wide-open fields. Continue to follow the wind as it carries the distant clouds across the far blue sky. Close your eyes and listen. Can you hear sounds from every direction? From close by? Far away? Can you tell if the source of any sound is moving?

While walking or sitting, be aware of the air within you and all around you. Feel that everything you see and hear is a part of you.

Let my mind become silent,
And my thoughts come to rest.
I want to be
All that is before me.
In self-forgetfulness,
I become everything.

—*Joseph Cornell*

Henry David Thoreau said, "You cannot perceive beauty but with a serene mind." If your mind needs quieting, bring it to a calm focus by repeating this poem—or a personal favorite of your own—as you walk.

The birds have vanished in the sky,
and now the last cloud drains away.
We sit together, the mountain and I
until only the mountain remains.

—Li Po

*I*n Li Po's poem, the birds and clouds are the restless thoughts that keep us from experiencing life more deeply. The mountain represents the richness of life that is always there, and which is truly seen only when our thoughts are still. The following activity will help you quiet your thoughts and "see the mountain" better.

Calmly gaze at a beautiful scene before you. Observe the natural flow of your breath. Do not control it in any way. Each time you inhale, think "Still." Each time you exhale, think "ness." Repeating "Still...ness" with each complete breath helps focus the mind and prevents your attention from wandering from the present moment.

This world is so beautiful
that I can hardly believe it exists.

—*Ralph Waldo Emerson*

*Emerson also said, "Though we travel the
world over to find the beautiful, we must carry
it with us or we find it not..."*

Discover the harmony within you and you will feel the harmony that runs through nature.

—Joseph Cornell

Emerson said, "A beautiful soul always dwells in a beautiful world."

"The care of rivers is not a question of rivers, but of the human heart."

—*Tanaka Shozo*

Only by uplifting our consciousness can we ever truly change the way we look at and relate to the world around us.

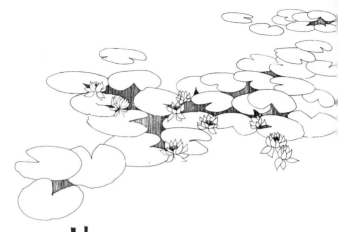

Until he extends the circle
of his compassion to all
living things, man will
not himself find peace.

—*Albert Schweitzer*

*T*he ability to empathize with other forms of life enlarges our own. As our awareness of all life grows, so does our happiness. Consciously "extend the circle of your compassion" to all the forms of life around you. You will feel the delight that comes from living fully aware of the largeness of life.

Love the world as your own self,
then you can truly care
for all things.

—*Lao Tsu*

Two:
Special Nature Experiences

The trail is beautiful...be still.

—*Lakota*

I live not in myself, but I became a
portion of all around me ... Are not
the mountains, waves and skies
a part of me and of my soul,
as I of them?

—*Lord Byron*

A teacher in the Southwest once asked the children in his class to draw a picture of themselves. He recalled, "The American children completely covered the paper with a drawing of their body, but my Navajo students drew themselves very differently. They made their bodies much smaller and included the nearby mountains, canyon walls, and dry desert washes. To the Navajo, the environment is as much a part of who they are as are their own arms and legs."

Nature's greatest gift to us is the understanding that we are part of something larger than ourselves. In nature, our self-identity expands, and so does our concern for the well-being of all.

The following activities help us affirm and experience our oneness with all life.

Expanding Circles

*F*ind a panoramic view with an interesting foreground. If possible, look for a scene that includes natural movement, like a rippling lake or swaying trees.

Sit down. Close your eyes and become aware of your body.

Now open your eyes, and extend your awareness beyond the body a few feet to the nearby grasses, rocks and insects. Feel yourself moving and becoming alive in them. Try to feel that you are in everything you see, just as much as you are in your own body. Do this for a couple of minutes. Whenever your mind wanders, bring it back gently to what's before you.

Broaden your awareness to include the nearby shrubs and trees. Continue to extend your visual *awareness in small stages, to ten, twenty, and thirty feet away. Feel that everything you see is a part of you.*

Extend your awareness out fifty yards, a hundred yards, to the distant ridges, and into the vast blue sky.

All the while, hold onto the awareness of yourself in the closest things near you, as well as in the far hills and sky. Allow your attention to flow spontaneously to whatever captures your interest. Feel that you are in everything.

THE BIRDS OF THE AIR

Love is expansive and includes everything as its own. Reflect on the meaning of the following poem, "Birds of the Air." As you say each line, project your thoughts of goodwill and love to all.

Nature responds to us when we approach it with love and respect. Through activities like this one, we can discover a beautiful, living, reciprocal relationship with all life.

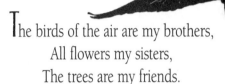

The birds of the air are my brothers,
All flowers my sisters,
The trees are my friends.

All living creatures,
Mountains and streams,
I take unto my care.

For this green earth is our Mother
Hidden in the sky is the Spirit above.
I share one Life with all who are here;
To everyone I give my love,
To everyone I give my love.

—*Joseph Cornell*

A Walk with the Creator

Imagine that you and the Creator are walking together. Share with the Creator every impression you see and hear, just as you would with a treasured friend. Gaze at the clouds and enjoy them together. Take delight in the birds singing all around, and bask in the sun's warm rays. Thank the Creator for the joy and beauty you feel.

Feel the love of God. . . . You will find a magic, living relationship uniting the trees, the sky, the stars, all people, and all livings things; and you will feel a oneness with them.

—*Paramahansa Yogananda*

Three:
PERSONAL REFLECTIONS

There is more to life than
increasing its speed.

—Gandhi

A friend was standing on a hotel balcony one night in Mexico, enjoying the city lights spread out before him. Suddenly a power failure plunged everything into darkness—everything, that is, but the stars, which he hadn't seen because the glow of the city had overpowered their subtle light.

Similarly, if we aren't careful, the rush of modern life can overpower our awareness of the beauty of nature, and the beauty of our own lives. The secret is to always keep part of our selves focused on the heavens.

What Would You Like to Remember?

During your walk, you probably discovered many new things about nature and about yourself. To help you reflect more on your experiences, choose a word that describes what you are feeling right now. Use each letter of the word to begin a line of a poem. For example, if you felt a sense of peace and chose the word "serene," your first line would begin with an "S."

S <u>tillness all around me</u>

E _____

R _____

E _____

N _____

E _____

Use the Notes section at the back of this book to work on your poem, then write your finished copy here.

_____

_____

_____

_____

_____

_____

_____

_____

_____

Four:

SHARING WITH OTHERS

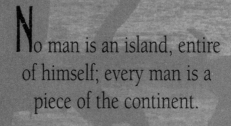

No man is an island, entire
of himself; every man is a
piece of the continent.

—*John Donne*

These activities will help you share the inspiring quotations in this book.

THE TRAIL OF BEAUTY

Find a beautiful trail and place the quotations alongside it, at locations where the words and surroundings complement each other. Send people down the trail, one at a time.

You can print 8 1/2 x 11-inch trail signs from the Sharing Nature website at www.sharingnature.com/beauty. This site gives further information about this and other activities. Don't miss the Trail of Beauty experience that will take you through some of the most stunning scenery in the American West.

Nature Meditations

Make copies of the quotations and place them in a pile. Have the members of your group look for one or two quotations that are especially meaningful for them. Allow a few minutes for reflection, then call the group together to tell about their experiences. (To learn more about this activity, see Sharing Nature with Children II, pages 113-114.)

Find The Best Place

Have a child draw a picture on a quotation card, then ask him or her to look for the best location for the quotation. With a group of children, make a trail connecting all the "best places." Use simple quotations, such as "This world is so beautiful that I can hardly believe it exists."

Acknowledgments

Henry David Thoreau said, "My profession is to be always on the alert to find God in nature…" I've always shared Thoreau's interest, so much so, that in college I majored in nature awareness. I am deeply indebted to J. Donald Walters for helping me understand how to experience life more deeply. In addition, I would like to thank Roy Simpson for sharing with me the original concept that inspired the Trail of Beauty activity. Thanks to George Beinhorn and Sheila Rush for their editorial comments. And I especially thank Anandi for her many invaluable suggestions and insights.

About the Author

Joseph Cornell is one of the world's leading nature educators. His books have been translated into more than seventeen languages, and his workshops have been attended by thousands of people around the globe. Mr. Cornell works closely with the Japan Nature Game Association, an organization of over 7,000 educators and leaders that uses and promotes the Sharing Nature philosophy and activities in Southeast Asia. As founder of Sharing Nature Worldwide, Joseph travels frequently to give programs. Mr. Cornell lives at Ananda Village near Nevada City, California, a community based on the teachings of Paramhansa Yogananda, where he teaches meditation. You can find out more about Joseph's work and his books at www.sharingnature.com, or by contacting the Sharing Nature Foundation at 14618 Tyler Foote Road, Nevada City, CA 95959, phone/fax: 530-478-7650, or email info@sharingnature.com.

Resources from Joseph Cornell

Sharing Nature with Children I (20th Anniversary edition)
Sharing Nature with Children II (formerly Sharing the Joy of Nature)
Listening to Nature
Journey to the Heart of Nature
John Muir: My Life with Nature
Ocean Animal Clue Game
Rainforest Animal Clue Game
Sharing Nature Walk (audio tape)
Sharing Nature with Children (video)
Sharing Nature Foundation website, www.sharingnature.com
All resources available from Dawn Publications

CREDITS

Photographs
Robert Frutos: cover, 8, 9, 26, 31, 34, 38, 42,46, 53, 56, 58, 62, 63
Akio Shoji: 5, 12, 16, 53
Joseph Cornell: 48, 49
Rodney Polden: 10

Illustrations
Elizabeth Ann Kelley: 24, 44
Sierra Nevada Natural History, Storer, T. and Usinger, R.L.,
University of California Press, 1971: 70, 71
Diane Iverson: 14, 18, 23, 28, 41

Quotations
Muir (p.3): Muir, John, Steep Trails, Houghton Mifflin Co., New
    York, 1918 p. 128.
Thoreau (p. 13): as quoted in Epstein, R., and Phillips, S., eds., The
    Natural Man: A Thoreau Anthology, Quest Books, Wheaton,
    Illinois, 1978 p. 82.
Walters (p.18): Walters, J. Donald, Do It Now!, Crystal Clarity
    Publishers, Nevada City, California, 1995 p. 33.
Navajo Indians (p. 19): Cronyn, George W., ed., American Indian
    Poetry, Fawcett Publishing Company, 1918 p. 77.
Carver (p. 22): Clark, G., The Man Who Talks with the Flowers,
    Macalester Park Publishing Co., St. Paul, Minnesota, 1939 p. 22.

Muir (p. 25): Muir, J., My First Summer in the Sierra, Houghton Mifflin, New York, 1916, pp. 211, 319.

Winnebago Indians (p. 28): McLuhan, T.C., Touch the Earth, Touchstone Books (Simon & Schuster, Inc.), New York, 1971, p. 5.

Austin (p. 30): Austin, Mary, Earth Horizon, Mary Austin, Houghton Mifflin Co., New York, 1932.

Walters (p. 31): Walters, J. Donald, Do It Now!, Crystal Clarity Publishers, Nevada City, California, 1995, p. 35.

Muir (p. 32): Wolfe L. M., ed., John of the Mountains: The Unpublished Journals of John Muir, Houghton Mifflin Co., New York, 1938, p. 92.

Cornell (p. 35): Cornell, J., Listening to Nature, Dawn Publications, Nevada City, California, 1987, p. 33.

Shozo (p. 42): Strong, K., Ox Against the Storm, University of British Columbia Press, Vancouver, Canada, 1977.

Cornell (p. 55): Cornell, J., Listening to Nature, Dawn Publications, Nevada City, California, 1987, p. 25.

Yogananda (p.57): Self-Realization Fellowship, Inner Reflections, 1997 Engagement Calendar, April 28 - May 4.

Every effort has been made to locate the publishers of the material quoted in the text. Grateful acknowledgment is made to all of these publishers for permissions given. Omissions brought to our attention will be credited in subsequent printings.

NOTES

NOTES

Nature Awareness Books from Dawn Publications

Spirit Animals, by Victoria Covell. When you encounter a wild animal, either physically or in your dreams, they bring a valuable message. This book presents the primal symbolism of 24 species, and tells you how to hear and understand animal wisdom or guidance.

Play Lightly on the Earth, by Jacqueline Horsfall, written especially with 3 to 9 year olds in mind, is packed with original activities with an emphasis on creative thinking, problem-solving, and skill development—all in the guise of play.

Especially for Children

Stickeen, John Muir and the Brave Little Dog, by John Muir as retold by Donnell Rubay, an illustrated version of the story of how John Muir and Stickeen handle the challenge and are changed by it.

Places of Power, by Michael DeMunn, just as native people have always known that places in nature have power, this book explores how children can become attuned to their own place of power.

Wonderful Nature, Wonderful You, by Karin Ireland, shows how nature can be a great teacher, reminding us to do things at our own pace and to bloom where we are planted.

Do Animals Have Feelings Too? by David L. Rice, is an illustrated collection of true observations of animal behaviors, both heart-warming and thought-provoking, showing the variety of animal feelings.

Dawn Publications is dedicated to inspiring a deeper understanding and appreciation for all life on Earth. To order, or for a copy of our catalog, please call 800-545-7475, or visit our web site at www.dawnpub.com.